About the Author

Meg James is a mother, a poet, a writer, a librarian, a witch, a woman, a disaster, a goddess, and above all- a human. She lives her life as she pleases, which sometimes gets her into trouble. But mostly, it just makes her free. She's glad you exist and she's glad you're reading this. Welcome to a wild and beautiful life.

Past Lives & Present Wounds

Meg James

Past Lives & Present Wounds

Olympia Publishers
London

www.olympiapublishers.com
OLYMPIA PAPERBACK EDITION

Copyright © Meg James 2023

The right of Meg James to be identified as author of
this work has been asserted in accordance with sections 77 and 78 of
the Copyright, Designs and Patents Act 1988.

All Rights Reserved

No reproduction, copy or transmission of this publication
may be made without written permission.
No paragraph of this publication may be reproduced,
copied or transmitted save with the written permission of the publisher,
or in accordance with the provisions
of the Copyright Act 1956 (as amended).

Any person who commits any unauthorised act in relation to
this publication may be liable to criminal
prosecution and civil claims for damage.

A CIP catalogue record for this title is
available from the British Library.

ISBN: 978-1-80439-316-1

This is a work of fiction.
Names, characters, places and incidents originate from the writer's
imagination. Any resemblance to actual persons, living or dead, is
purely coincidental.

First Published in 2023

Olympia Publishers
Tallis House
2 Tallis Street
London
EC4Y 0AB

Printed in Great Britain

Dedication

For the dreamers. For C and O. But mostly, for myself.

Acknowledgements

There are too many to thank personally who deserve it, but here's a short list of those who made this possible: To Mom, for always demanding more when I wrote. To Dad, for saying "I'll help if I can" at the right time. To Matthew, for never faltering in his belief that I would do this, and for everything else. I love you. To C and O, for always making me laugh and for making me a better person. Mama wrote a book, boys! And to those who taught me the lessons. I took what you gave me and made it beautiful- even when it hurt. Watch me shine.

Introduction

These are disastrous times. The past two years have been almost impossible for all of us, bringing everyone I know to their knees at one point or another.

Within these pages are the best, the most raw, the most honest of my words over the past two years. You won't find COVID-19 referenced more than once or twice, however, because these years have held disasters of a far more personal and private nature. While the world stood still for a virus no one saw coming, my own world had crumbled and fallen into dust.

These words are the shattered pieces. These words are the rebuilding.

There are four parts to this collection, loosely tracking the course of two years of my life. Looking back and trying to decide how to organize this collection, I knew I had done it for myself when I wrote the words. This is a journey, and I can track my progress through it section by section. I hope you can see the journey as well, and maybe take one of your own.

My journey isn't over. Neither is yours.

Part I:

These Fragile Things

and now that you don't have to be perfect, you can be good.
-john steinbeck

Here at the End of All These Things

By the time their light reaches our eyes,
We are admiring a graveyard of stars.
The night sky wheels with lost souls
Traveling one final journey for a farewell
Before there was ever a hello.
Do not tell me endings cannot be beautiful.

29 March 2020

These Fragile Things

I am
                        Becoming
A cacophony of stereotypes-

        A symphony of clashing
Strengths, desires, needs-

I am
                        Moving

Through the boundless emptiness
      Of all these human beings-

And I
        Am breaking;

I am broken,
        A china-doll held
    Together by fraying string-

But I am
                        Stronger
      Than the sum
           Of all these fragile things.

                                        12 November 2018

Ad Orare

I leave behind a wine-dark stain
No matter how hard I try
A smudged reminder on everything my lips touch

(I have a mouth made for sinning)

On my knees in the dark
Painted words in the back of my throat
Taste of salt and feel like heaven
Unchained even as I choke on silence

I speak smooth as honey but burn like whiskey
Bruisèd crimson barbs from a soft, curved bow
Even I don't know if I am sweet or bitter,
But *darling* and *damn* taste the same

Licking temptation from a fingertip until
My hands are clean, I know
How to grip destiny between my teeth
And the weight of innocence on my tongue
But both leave red on a white porcelain cup

(I'd rather taste pomegranate than peach)

28 April 2020

Uncivilized Hearts

I have an insufferable urge to be reckless-
To ask the questions no one dares speak;
To walk the roads no one dares tread;
To sing loudly in all the places
Silence hangs heavy and demands respect.

I am filled to the brim,
Poised to overflow into aching chaos;
Cacophony of conflicting desires
Pulling me into thousands of pieces
Of fast-fading stardust.

I will give my heart away for
The price of a dance, a story, a song;
In drips of blood from outstretched fingers,
So overwhelmed with the urge to know
Another being like I know myself that I don't see
I am burning the very gift I am offering.

Uncivilized hearts cannot be tamed.
Reckless souls cannot be controlled.
And storms cannot be calmed-
Merely named.

3 March 2020

Beautiful Things

Beautiful things don't seek attention.
They merely exist, being themselves,
And we are caught in their gravity to orbit their reality-
Held in place but at a distance
To look and yearn and never touch.
Does the moon desire to drink the earth's cool blue waters
Like I ache to taste
The color of your eyes and the texture of your hair
In early morning light,
My sheets tangled around you and my pillow
Held captive as you dream?
Beautiful things merely exist,
Wholly themselves and unbothered
By the attention of those who cannot help but stare.

                                                20 March 2020

Storms Are Named for People Like Us

You and I are nothing-
Wildness wearing human skin.
You are the booming crash of thunder;
I am the weight of the rising wave;
And together we are the storm.

26 March 2020

Lost Boys

Once we were kings,
Running barefoot in the grass of our wild domain,
Unconquered rulers of a country as wide as our dreams
And smaller than our place in the universe.
Heedless of the passing hours stretching into years
And drawing on inevitably toward the instant
We cast aside our sunny crowns,
We raced recklessly through the misspent moments
Of our youth, wishing away the golden days believing
That we would always be savage royalty,
Kings of the dusty, well-trod path
Between your world and mine.

                                                26 March 2020

I would write you poetry if I knew your name

there is witchcraft in her lips
I watch the way they shape words,
red and bright and quirking upward
in a smile for her adoring crowd
I wonder if the color on them would
stain mine, if I tried to drink
her magic warm from the source
would her words taste of cherries
or of blood,
stolen from her throat
        to mine?

26 April 2020

Souls and Stars Are Made the Same

I swing wildly between believe
I am destined for great things
And that I am nothing.
The truth lies somewhere in the middle.
We are all merely stardust,
Drifting in the galaxy and longing
For home.

24 March 2020

Losing My Religion

There is a church on every street corner here,
Their signs promising salvation.
I would like to believe the words on their white lighted
backgrounds,
But I spent countless Sundays of my youth sitting
In hard wooden pews singing hymns by rote,
And I have tasted heaven more surely
In the way the word *fuck* feels in my mouth
Or the stinging needles leaving an imagine
On the altar of the temple my lost soul was born in
Than in any off-key piano note bidding me to rise.
I have seen more angels in a traffic jam
Than I've ever seen in dusty stained-glass light,
And the voices on the radio hold far more truth
Than street corner signs proclaiming good news
That no one stops to hear.

27 March 2020

Between the Stars and Tides

Have you ever noticed that
Galaxies and sea foam are the same?
We are all floating through the abyss
Seeking something that feels like home.
Maybe gravity is just the pattern of
Stardust in your eyes, and maybe
The tightness of my lungs is you
Drowning in the ocean in mine.
Someday I will understand why souls
Can't touch the way fingertips do,
But I will never comprehend how
To live my life content on the ground
When we are trapped
Between the stars and the tides;
Or how to settle for the ordinary
When such a universe is mine.

27 June 2020

things you'll never see

dancing in the dark, eyes closed
despite the way the only light in this quiet house
is from headlights on the road outside
I want to run, so I turn up the volume
on a slow-dance song and sing along
spinning alone until I forget
I am bound by skin and time, focusing
on the single truth in a galaxy
of slowly-imploding lies-
every moment passes eventually
even this one

1 April 2020

Infinite

How can I be exhausted and yet
Overflowing with energy?
I am sick of being bound
Within these four walls of skin and stone
When I am made of galaxies.
A golden chain is still a leash.
If you bottle the sea and
Bring it back to decorate your mantelpiece
You will wake to find yourself drowning.
These bonds are limited but I am infinite,
A tired star dreaming in the storm-tossed sea,
And someday I will wake to burn free.

2 April 2020

You Cannot Own What Comes with the Tides

I loved a selkie in a past life

       I stole his pelt, smooth and warm,
and wrapped myself around him in its place

                 he loved me back
                 of that I'm sure

but selkies are married to the sea
       and I am in love with her too
and even a selkie and a sea-witch are
not immune to the steady erosion of the tides

       I loved a selkie in a past life,
and both of us returned to the sea

                                     30 May 2020

There is a place between asleep and awake

Liquid dreams flow through my fingers
You cannot hold on to dust.
Sometimes I am weightless and floating
Made of impossible things and an eternity of effort
Sometimes I am dust.
There are rivers flowing through the universe
Rivers flowing through my veins
We are all made up of dreams
We are all buried in the dust.

30 August 2020

Time Flows from Empty Cups

Can I drink the blood of a god?

I have sucked nectar and honey from bruised lips;
Licked wine from fingertips adorned in jewels and gold.
I have feasted on the flesh of men
And consumed the darkest delight from wayward hearts.

For a mortal, I am hungry.
Is it savagery or immortality I crave?

I will taste the blood of a god,
And let some other starving mortal
Drink it from my lips or lap it from my palm
Knowing as all desperate savages that
Eternity is never far away.

16 July 2020

tell me, Father, why we speak sins and silence sacraments

What a burden it is to be good

            Wouldn't you rather be free
            Dancing in the shadowy spaces
            Between light and dark
            And full of the knowledge that you are
            Wild and finite and uncaged

    How much better to be a raging storm
    Illuminated by lightening and baptized in rainfall
    Than a cloudless summer sky
    Passive and perfect and forgotten
    When the last rays have slipped below the horizon

Too much sun bleaches even the brightest colors white

Saints have names, but no longer voices

                                  17 June 2020

unworthy offerings

I long to be ruined more than to be loved
I have been loved before, and needed

I will suffocate on this pristine pedestal,
Surrounded by empty promises and unlit candles.
                      An altar stained with wax and wine
                      Knows the agony of devotion.

I am ready to be craved; to be
Stripped down to my barest parts, raw and bleeding,
And drunk to the marrow of my storm-tossed soul-
Left bruised and marred by devouring hands and worshiping lips

    In crumbling temples old gods sleep,
      The land still rich with the memory of desperate pleas
        And stone worn smooth and cracked from bended knees.
Stained glass purity is cold and lonely;
Hallowed halls echo with the weight of silent reverence.

I do not want to be holy
I want to be destroyed

                                            30 April 2020

Not All Who Wander

You cannot be lost if you can see the sky.
The sun rises in the east and sets in the west;
Polaris points North, and all else follows.

I cannot be lost, no matter how far I wander,
Because I can look to the sky and see
The setting sun or the scattered diamond stars,
And I know that somewhere waiting for me
There is a sunset over quiet water
A crescent moon and familiar laughter
And a warm welcome as sure as
The sun rises in the east and
Sets in the west.

Even birds come back to the nest.

29 March 2020

Dangerous Things

I have run from wolves my whole life
Skipping from stars to hours in order
To cross the endless, foaming void
Ahead of snapping jaws and sharp teeth.
My path will never be straight or clear or bright
But twisting in shadows and filled with
Dangerous things. I am one of them.
Do I run from wolves, or are they chasing me?
Time stands still in the forest of my dreams
And eternity is long time to spend
With your enemies. Maybe the wolves
Are running from me.

9 July 2020

We Could Be an Epic Story, Couldn't We?

I look at him and I see
All the sins I never had the courage
To commit.

He makes me reckless and urgent,
Hungry for more than the steady barrage of days
Leading inevitably to the end of time itself.

I feel as though, if I loved him and he loved me,
He would leave me breathless and broken
On his way to the next adventure,
And I would thank him for giving me wings
As they burned to ash in mid-flight.

26 May 2020

Forgotten Tales

I wrote these stories for you.
Ink-stained fingers flowing over white pages
Were not enough, so I
Dip my pen into my heart
And scrawl fantasies
On the blank canvas of my body,
Knowing you will read only the lines
On my thighs and believe you are the hero.
(I have never needed saving.)

23 April 2020

It Wasn't Icarus Who Fell

His name tastes heavy on my tongue
As his hands move soft and sure
Along my spine, giving me wings.
In the shadows we fly, he and I,
And in the blazing sunlight
We turn to weighted ash
And fall silent.

22 April 2020

Gods and Monsters

Last night I dreamt of gods and monsters.
Things moved in the shadows and in the blinding light
And I realized it didn't matter
Which you were or which I am-
Dark or light, I could not see.
God or monster, I am still me.

7 May 2020

The Tides Rise and So Shall I

My mother found a whole sand dollar once,
Walking the sea shore.
She keeps it in her dresser, and as a child
I wondered what it was like to be that lucky,
Sneaking a look and a cautious touch during chores.

It took years and mistakes for me realize
We forge our own luck with our own power,
And I am not the sand-dollar type anyway.

I am hag-stones and broken shells on a stained altar,
Giving an offering to the ocean with my morning coffee,
Receiving back something greater than luck-
Strength.

29 May 2020

A Gathering Storm

I have an overwhelming feeling that something
Is about to happen.
The universe is holding its breath,
Gathering itself like the clouds before a summer storm.
The omens are there-
Birds of three and four, soaring together;
Candle flame flickering bright;
Stones of destiny and success and happiness.
Something is coming, the wind whispers.
Something good, the sun promises,
Rays caressing my face like a lover's tough.
Something good. You have only to wait.

6 April 2020

Part II:

Adrenaline in A Minor

you can stand me up at the gates of hell, but I won't back down.
-tom petty

Social Distancing

I want to have half-drunk 2 am conversations
At noon, deep thoughts and smothered laughter
As if every soul I meet knows mine already.

Small talk is only empty, meaningless words,
But if you were to tell me why that
One line of your favorite song
Makes your heart ache every time,
I could listen for hours.

But 2 am conversations
Are not meant for the bright light of day
And strangers don't seem to care
That storms make me feel wild and free and alive
More than sunshine ever could.

So I nod and smile and stay quiet,
And I don't ask why you inked your skin
Or what your best memory is,
Because noon friends are not 2 am friends,
And I don't know how to be anything less
Than all or nothing.

30 March 2020

Summer Lies

I don't like how my knees look in shorts,
So for years I didn't wear them.
Summer heat crushing my shoulders,
Thick and palpable; a living beast's
Hot breath on my sweating skin,
And I would say I was fine with a smile
As bright and empty as the cloudless sky.
(I learned to lie young.
I learned to be good at it.)
Now as I button maroon shorts-
Stacked waist, ending high on my pale thighs-
I wrinkle my nose at my legs in the mirror.
(The truth is, I still don't like how my knees look.)
The truth is, I'd rather be happy than beautiful.

24 May 2020

Unlearned Lessons

There's a lot of things my parents taught me,
But as I get older I've noticed some information is missing.

Like how buying condoms will always make me blush,
But buying tampons never should-
Though they did teach me how to punch properly
If some jerk tried to give me shit about anything.

They did their best to prepare me for "the real world"
But how in the hell were they supposed to
Teach me to recognize the wolf in his eyes
When I didn't show them the sheep in mine?

Fabric softener is useless and damaging.
So are endless "I'm sorrys" for the same damn thing.

Maybe my dad taught me how to shake a man's hand,
But he didn't know that sometimes
Pretty girls make mine tremble more than my anxiety ever could,
So how am I supposed to tell him
I'm not exactly straight
When I hardly know who appeals to me?

How do I file taxes when I can't ask my ex anything
Because he taught me my voice doesn't matter,
But technically we're still married and
One of us has to claim the kids, don't we?

Sometimes I wish it was as easy to ask my mom
If she'll still love me if I don't believe what she believes
As it is to tell her I have no idea
Where to go to get a copy of my baby's birth certificate
Or how to keep my composure when the man I married
Is yelling at me for telling him
I don't agree to something.

You see, it's not the same
When you love someone as much as I love them
And you know you're going to disappoint them if you say
"Hey. Mom? Dad? I love you, and I'm not ok."

Hey, guys. Who do I call when my tires need to be rotated?
Love you. Call me back.

25 July 2020

words can bleed and ink can cut

I keep a list of cages
Scrawled on my abdomen.
Their bars are invisible
But the locks are solid,
Made of every word and gesture
That puts bounds on who I am
Supposed to be.

Hidden behind my lips are the keys,
And one by one I am
Shaping them into reality-
Giving them form from the blood
Running from my mouth
With every pointed word.

Someday, I will be free.
But the list is burned
Into my flesh by ink and sorrow,
And I will carry the memory of
My cages in scars
The whole world may see.

12 October 2020

If I am to be a devil, I will dance in the flames

This holy ground burns my feet.
I will not beg for love.
I tread the water's edge
To cool the flames,
Dancing through the pain to
The rhythm of the waves.
And all alone, I let burn
Every expectation of gods or men
Until what remains, strong and free,
Is only what I dream.
Worship is for those who do not love themselves,
And you were never a god to me.

26 June 2020

Is It Vanity or Loneliness?

Once upon a time my room was
Filled with pictures of you.
(We photograph that which we are afraid to lose.)
 I'm scrolling through my camera roll
And I realize- for years now,
It's been full of pictures of me.

14 July 2020

After a Storm

I know you never imagined
Forever had an expiration date
Or daydreams had a timer counting down
The moments until they disappear.

I always thought thirty meant having
My life in order, but I'm standing
Close to that precipice and honestly
I know less now than I knew a decade ago,
When I looked in your eyes and
Saw an endless stretch of tomorrows.

Somehow it has become today;
And I'm no longer interested
In forever or eternity or even tomorrow.
There is only now, alone in my house
With paint on my hands and music in my ears,
And today is enough for me.

4 August 2020

Love & War

Your name is a foul taste, heavy on my tongue;
Lingering behind bared teeth and lips curled in a sneer.

> *(First kiss: soft, sweet, hesitant. A question.*
> *Last kiss: hard, rough. Your lips an army,*
> *Besieging the fortress of my mouth, and*
> *It falls, it falls, it falls.)*

Blood stained teeth sink into the tip of my tongue
And the tang of copper washes your name away.

> *(Maybe you breached the fortress walls,*
> *But savagery lingers behind soft lips and now*
> *You'll fall, you'll fall, you'll fall.)*

2 August 2020

Bad Girls Do It Better

they say good girls go to heaven

how sad I am for them
all that time spent with weight crushing your soul
the gossamer strands of *goodness* binding more
surely than *badness* ever could

and for what? In the end
they reach the pearly gates only to discover
more of the velvet shackles and sinking burden

it's no wonder all the angels look unhappy
what a terrible way to live, so
afraid of dying your whole life becomes a waste

5 August 2020

Is It the World I Hate or Myself?

Sometimes I think anger is
The only reason I'm alive.

My body is fed by rage and watered by hate
And while I forget to eat
And fail to sleep
And spend my time in mute silence
With unuttered arguments filling my ears,
Still I am here.
Still I am here.
Still,
I am here.

I know damn well the blood on my bared teeth
Is my own-
But oh, it tastes sweet.

9 October 2020

[destruction is better than suffocation]

>The moon is lovely,
>But it merely reflects
>Another's light.
>Be a star
>And shine-
>*Even when you explode.*

4 October 2020

Mercy

Do not mistake my compassion for weakness-
Rust and bloodstains look the same.
Though a hand is extended, it need not be soft.
While my heart may bleed, it is
Forged from steel and tempered in hardship,
And if you choose to strike
You will learn that kindness is not often tame.

                                              12 September 2020

Adrenaline in A Minor

My head is full of all these
Imaginary conversations and made up scenarios,
    A riotous cacophony of what is, what isn't,
What might be
        hidden beneath the surface-

It's hard to breathe when I'm
    Drowning in my own mind.

    Silence isn't golden; it's bursting
With possible meaning and the only way
    To know with certainty is to ask-

But my lungs are full of blood,
        Not oxygen.

    All the clamor in my ears
Blocks out the words I see spoken,
    And I don't need anyone else
    to destroy me.

I'm doing it just fine on my own.

8 October 2020

Heard on High

No one expects an angel to set the world on fire,
But there's a reason their first words are "fear not."

Perfection is terrifying,
And I almost destroyed myself trying.

Thousands of eyes strip my soul bare;
Lay out the essence of who I am
And chose what's good and what's sin.

I never liked being naked-
All my flaws on display for you to
Point them out and call me unworthy.

A flaming sword might cauterize the wound,
But just because it doesn't bleed, doesn't
Mean it doesn't hurt.

If I bled at your feet,
You would blame me for the stain.

It's easy to forget Lucifer still has wings.

7 August 2020

(do not let them try to define you)

I am not as simple as they wanted me to be.
I do not fit into their tiny boxes,
Because I am made of contrasting
curves and razor-sharp edges,
And they do not lay neatly into a clear plastic case.

Square pegs and round holes
Are still too confining-
I am more than my shape,
More than my features,
More than my loves and my hates
And my beliefs-

I am not as simple as they wanted me to be.
(And neither are you.)

13 October 2020

11:36 {stay the hell away from me}

Gravity is something I feel in my throat.
I've switched personalities like trying on clothes
Yet sometimes I wonder why nobody knows
Who I am.

My hands won't stop shaking; please don't get to close.
I'm dying to know you; I'd die to be known
But I can't remember what holds me together-
Am I bleeding or crying tonight?

Alone on these sheets and hearing my heartbeat
I can't help but question if time has been broken
Cause surely this night has been going for
Years-

But it isn't the sunrise that's turning the skies red
It's me with a paintbrush at 2:45,
Trying to figure out why I'm alive,
And sometimes the only thing holding me down
Is the echoing sound of each passing minute
And hour
And year.

I think I want to be here....

But gravity's only a word
That I heard on the radio
When I barely knew who I was
Or who I wanted to be.

16 October 2020

Please Remit Payment by Date Below

I pay my bills with Disney villain stamps.

My parents taught me to always
Think for myself,
But now when I speak
They give me concerned looks
And ask where I'm getting these ideas.

I think I'm supposed to have a voice
But only as long as it blends into the melody,
And I don't like singing harmony.

Sometimes I try to be a good girl,
But these days I like the villains
Better than the princesses,
And my voice is too strong for the chorus anyway-
So I'll pay my bills with Disney villain stamps
And my dues in cautious words.

I'm more afraid of going silent than growing up.

15 October 2020

Into the Great Wide Open [your heroes are sometimes your friends]

Rebellion never sat well on my shoulders
Unless it was petty-
The worthless kind that let me feel reckless
But kept me utterly safe.
I think I'd be less afraid now if I'd taken more risks then,
But somehow I still find myself on the receiving end
Of dismayed concern and awkward silences all the same.

There's someone I know who wears rebellion
Like it's inked into her skin-
So confident in her refusal to be shoved
Into spaces too small and confined
For the wildness she's made of
That it practically sings in her movements,
A chorus of *'I'm free, I'm free, I'm me'*
Behind every laugh and fuck-you shrug.

I asked her how she does it once.
She said by being just like me.

Maybe I've always been a rebel without a clue,
And now I'm only discovering
The reckless soul that's been lurking
Under the surface all along.

Someday maybe rebellion will cling to me
Like a well-worn leather jacket,
And I will radiate darkness and light
In a dazzling display of *different* and *unknown*
That refuses to be dulled or directed,
And someone young and desperate will ask me how
I echo with wild in a world clamoring for tame.

Maybe someday I'll be able to say,
"By being like you."

25 October 2020

Exit Holes

Maybe I'm the one who made the decisions,
At the end of the day,
And I know I did it all to myself.

The entry wound is smaller than the exit hole,
So no one will look at the shredded
Devastation of my life and see
How it all began with the things you said to me.

It's easier to say it was my decision
Than try to trace evidence back
When the bullet's gone.

I guess I'll hold the smoking gun.

22 October 2020

Ad Meridium

I know that I've said I have a mouth made for sin-
Wine-red lips and rug-burned knees,
The taste of pomegranate heavy on my tongue.

(I had Heaven between my teeth once,
Fresh and golden, the summer-sweet
Of juice and honey running down my chin)

Pale pink and rosy hues spread like dawn
Across my cheeks and I am confounded
By the thought that I am more than stained cups,
More than whisky and barbs and dark rooms-

(I never saw myself as sunrise and new beginnings;
Never thought I'd wonder if shit *and* sweetheart
Could both mean salvation*)*

I wonder if *soft* means more than skin on skin
And the silken touch of a bedsheet,
And if it would feel as good twinned around my body
When the night gets cold-

(Do I taste peach in the back of my throat?)

Maybe I can be both.

27 October 2020

Is There a French Tuck for Life?

Someone asked why I wore combat boots
And I didn't tell them
    Because I have been fighting my whole life

Style is slipping on someone else's skin
A tug on the hem and I am
No longer tugging on my father's hand
To ask for attention

I wear adulthood like my leather jacket
Suddenly I'm tougher than all the battles
I'm facing

    I like the look of them,
I say with a shrug
    I don't ask if you like the look of me.

28 October 2020

My Mother's Child

I joke that my mother can get away with anything
But when I ask the most capable people I know
How do you do it?
All they seem to say is *'sink or swim'*

I'm swimming as hard as I can
But the shoreline keeps receding
And I'm bleeding into shark-infested waters

"Just ask for what you need"
I need
      A life preserver
           A boat
                 A *rope-*

See, ropes can strangle as fast as they can save
And I'm choking on the sea water
I'm swimming in

But my mother can get away with anything
And everyone says
      I'm just like her.

28 October 2020

Untitled 10/28

No one writes poetry about happy things

Sunshine and roses and dawn glows
Don't fill notebooks
And tear-stained pages of desperate dreams
Will always appeal to heartstrings

I don't want to write poetry anymore.

28 October 2020

This Isn't a Love Poem

       The day you left your shirt in my car
The air smelled of you the whole way home.

I refused to roll the windows down,
               But
      I blasted the music you gave me so loud
My ears hurt and I couldn't hear the words.

     I remember
Two solid hours of meandering conversation;
Your invitation an unexpected surprise-
        I think to us both.

           This is not a love poem,
And more than half of it
     is utter fiction anyway
But no one will know the difference

        Because I can weave tragedies from
Scraps of truth and one sideways glance

        Or twist three words and a daydream
            Into the greatest romance
The world will never know.

This isn't a love poem

But cigarette smoke used to fill me with dread.
    Now ash could pepper my shoulders
And I wouldn't even notice.

30 October 2020

Said//Unsaid

I can tell you
                                    I never wanted to be strong.

I never imagined I'd be someone
Who swiped blood from her knuckles and laughed through the pain,
Muttered exclamation of 'fuck me' the only sign
It hurts
                I can't tell you that's me asking, you know. Fuck me. Please.

I can say
                                    How I imagined I'd be.

A quiet life, where the only blood that spilled
Came from between my thighs,
And not from thin lines on my ribs, my lips, my arms

But passion and pain are one and the same,
And I can't do anything halfway-
Love or hate or something in between.
                                I can't say how good it feels to bleed.

I shouldn't tell you
                                How badly I want to be me.

                                          29 October 2020

Drizzling Mist (what's so unfair about it?)

Standing in my kitchen crying
On the phone with the girl I've never met
Who might be my best friend,
Wondering out loud why my father watched
With his arms crossed instead of even trying to hug me
As I cried in that same spot earlier

Life is unfair and I know that but the thing is
That doesn't mean it isn't hard and sometimes
I crack and sometimes I sob
Over trivial things like a broken heart
Or my house being a mess
Or my life falling apart

I do not understand what who I might someday chose to love
Has to do with anything but I'm learning
It's apparently everything

'I'm getting something to eat and going to bed'
I tell her 'I just needed to vent'

I just needed to feel cared about for half an hour
So I plunged my hands into the warm dishwater
And sobbed to the girl I've never met who knows
Me better sometimes than I know myself

I don't feel loved but the dishes are done
I don't feel strong but I do feel numb

1 November 2020

While Rome Burns (Election Night 2020)

You say *win or lose* like this is a game
This is my life
This is the lives of people I care for
This is the lives of people *you* care for
Served up on a platter for the world to kill or save

If this is a game, it's a bread-and-circus
And we are moments from the closed fist that takes
The loser's head

See, *win* or *lose*, we're already doomed
Because there are so many of you
Who say *it's only politics* and *can't we be friends despite our differences*

But it's our differences that leave me bleeding
From bitten lips and nails ripped off
Pacing the kitchen floor on election night
And trying not to hear my friends toying with our lives
What we're up against isn't as simple as *just another 4 years*

It's who we are
And it's not up to debate if I deserve to be me
But somehow you sit behind your keyboard and think
My future isn't dictated by a madman and a mob

This isn't ancient Rome
There's no gladiator ring but we are bleeding on our knees
The whole world wide-eyed as the emperor holds out his hand

We already know the outcome
So we're watching those of you in the stands
Because come tomorrow
No matter who *wins* and who *loses*
We have seen who views us as a game

                                        3 November 2020

; I am no longer linked to you

There is a semicolon after your name.
Maybe you didn't know that,
But I feel it every time it's spoken-
That pause, where something else ought to be
But isn't.
So the sentence drags on after it,
Slapped together with that semicolon
Because maybe then I won't notice the silence
Where my name used to follow yours.

31 October 2020

4:59pm, Friday

No one wants to talk about
Empty hours in cardboard rooms,
    Tick
        Tick
            Ticking
                In the silence
The only sign we aren't already dead,
But counting down the hours to it instead.

This is adulthood. We grow up; we go to work.

The air is full of thousands of painful jokes
    My boss is a nightmare-
        I work to afford my liquor-
            TGIF, amiright?
But no one is willing to point out
The incredible broken thing in the corner of the room
Holding the ticking clock with a puppet-master smile.

Maybe we shouldn't hate ¾ of our lives away,
    I say
Everyone laughs.

            Tick. Tick. Tick.

            30 October 2020

Maybe the Mayans Had It Right

Today a friend told me casually she never feels happy;
Then laughed at my 'same' a heartbeat later,
Stubbing out a cigarette and moving on like it was meaningless.

>We crack all the jokes we can to keep the chaos at bay,
>Laughing at stupid images and misspelled words,
>But have any of us felt alive since 2012 anyway?
>And isn't it sad that at some point,
>We all stopped really living and
>The world didn't even notice. It just kept going.

>All we listen to are sad songs; sad eyes behind
>Masks as we all swear this can't last,
>But 2020 won't seem to end and none of us
>Are convinced 2021 will be any different.

I didn't ask if she needed to talk because
I know it won't matter-

>This kind of sad a laugh won't cure.
>This kind of world leaves us all dying
>For something more.

>18 November 2020

Part III:

There's Something in the Water

My darling girl, when are you going to realize that being normal is not necessarily a virtue? It rather denotes a lack of courage.
-<u>practical magic</u>, alice hoffman

if i lose you, i'm losing everything

the water's on fire
I know it doesn't make sense for water to burn
but it doesn't make sense for me to be gone and you to be lost
but here we are

it's a raging blaze, spreading over cresting waves
and you'd think it'd be drowned like my grief but it's not
somehow it burns hotter than my skin where your fingers trailed
feather-light but fierce and possessive in flickering candlelight

the water's on fire
and I am afraid I never will be again

14 December 2020

Break Light

Someone on the radio sings about running
And the next thing I know I'm at a stop sign
At 5 in the morning. I should go left.
Nothing in my life has gone right
Since that midnight I decided to stop pretending
I was loved and everything
                              was perfect.

Somehow I'm always hoping the drive
Will change my mind but the truth is
False dawn and a Springsteen song isn't enough
To make me forget I'm letting down everyone
                              I give a shit about.

My turn signal blinks. Suddenly I'm seventeen and
Coming apart at the seams, so
                              I turn right.

It's just a stop sign, brake lights red in the rear view,
But I know better than to look back too long.
First dawn is false light and running away
Doesn't sit right with me after that first time.
                I should go left, but I guess I'm alright.

                                            25 November 2020

lightning and sand make glass, but lightning and water conduct electricity

> He's dangerous.
>> He says the same of you,
>> With your soft skin and soft lips,
>> Sly eyes and knowing smile.

> That's shallow.
>> So is fear.
>> It lays on your skin like
>> Scum on the surface of water,
>> But I promise you,
>> It does not sink in.

> Wildfire burns.
>> And the storm rages.
>> But rain soothes a burn,
>> And lightening and fire brighten the night.

> See? He's dangerous.
>> He says the same of you.

3 December 2020

Bleeding Ink

I haven't written a word in a week
I can feel it in my bones, how my joints hurt and knees creak
I usually pour it out onto the page
All these words captive in my rib cage can't speak
Can't breathe through thoughts like these

I'm burning paper houses,
Beaten up by cast stones and sidelong glances,
Collecting them in a too-full cup,
Drop by drop
Surface tension is only so strong
Someday it will overflow,
Gushing water washing away blood stains
Scrawled names filling empty space

I haven't written in over a week
My floor creaks differently at 2 am
I should hit my knees, but
Gods don't listen to words like these.

10 December 2020

Honey Fix Your Crown

I'm not a princess and never have been.

When I wore a big white dress I was a china-doll on a pedestal,
A pretty thing in gilded dreams to be admired from afar.
But they couldn't change my bare feet on solid earth,
Dirty and bruised as I whirled on the dance floor.

I am not a princess and I never will be.

I'm quick to roll up my sleeves and raise my chin.
Sharp tongue and sharp eyes might have been clouded once
But by the time the silk slid off and left cool air on bare skin
I already knew dreams and reality take work.
(He didn't.)

I'm not a princess and never wanted to be,
And I'll take these bruised knees and damp cheeks
Any day of the week. Pedestals and gowns aren't for those
Who dance barefoot over twig-strewn ground
And I never wanted to be pampered royalty anyway.

I'm not a fucking princess. I'm the Queen.

12 December 2020

coffee & calamities

& suddenly we're strangers,
Awkward small talk & awkward silences
Where once there'd have been whispered secrets & lingering touches.
I can still feel your fingertips bumping down the ridges of my spine,
Hear the ragged edge of your breath as you count each one.
& the silence creeps down slowly,
Settles like lead where you gave me butterflies.
But we sip morning coffee at the table
& pretend we're fine.

23 November 2020

pushing midnight

It's pushing midnight
(11:45; one of those times I regret I'm alive)
And I'm on the phone with a man but it isn't like that
He likes my mind and my personality, and it confuses me
How good that is for me, but I'm skipping part of the story
Cause I want to get to the end

(That's not important) the point is it's 11:55 and
Soon I won't be alive, at least not the old me.
Maybe in the morning I'll open my eyes
And be someone new who's glad she's alive
But pushing midnight is one of those times I regret
All of the choices and all of the lies and most of my life

(11:59)
I've got one minute to change my mind
But I'm surprised when the clock changes and I'm laughing,
Not crying

The new me is here (new me new year)-
I'm not fool enough to believe everything's changed
But the end of yesterday means I don't have to be the same
And at 12:05 that's a good enough reason to survive
Till I'm pushing midnight again

16 December 2020

the most powerful witch I know

I make the magic in my house.

Standing at my sink staring blindly at the lights on my Christmas tree,
I'm sipping coffee and wishing it wasn't morning.
It was midnight when I went down-
Six-thirty now and I've been awake awhile,
And I'm ready for the season to be over
But not really.

There's more to do behind the scenes
But my little one screams when he sees the lights
And my oldest can't decide if Halloween or Christmas time is better.

I make the magic in my house.
Everyday things like "the sun is cold behind his blanket of clouds"
To the stars in their eyes as they study the lights
I stopped seeing days ago, ever-delighted by the next surprise,

And I'm so exhausted but I remember
My mother's insanity every December and how we'd tease her-

I learned the magic from her.

17 December 2020

'tis the damn season, I guess

I plugged my Christmas tree in at 6:30 am
Now I'm crying in my kitchen
My hands are raw despite the lotion
That only happens when I'm so stressed I don't even know where to begin
'Tis the damn season, I guess

I plugged my Christmas tree in at 6:30 am
There's no other light but the coffee pot's beacon
For as much as I hate people I hate this feeling more
I'm tired of being alone, every night every morning everything in between
'Tis the damn season, I guess

I plugged my Christmas tree in at 6:30 am
I'm honestly not sure why I'm crying again
It isn't just the exhaustion, it isn't just the fucking stress
Taylor Swift said it best
'Tis the damn season, I guess

18 December 2020

is it exhaustion or peace

songs these days arent capitalized
and the words coming from my pen cant be bothered with punctuation
I think we're all just too damn exhausted for that shit
and I never thought lowercase would convey so much but
everything is so important, uppercase urgency
uppercase emergencies everywhere I turn
and I cant handle one more thing with an exclamation point
maybe thats why im writing unstructured lines
maybe thats why theres this fog on my mind
im tired of uppercase lives and uppercase lines
so this one isnt capitalized

18 December 2020

Christmas Eve

It's Christmas Eve and I've been up since 3:30 am.
Exhausted again, before the day's even begun,
And I don't want to spend Christmas alone
But I don't think I can stand one more emotional demand.
How is one person supposed to make all the magic happen?
I'm tired of holding it together, my sanity thin and ripping
Like taped-up pretty paper-
Frayed ribbon and bloodied fingers the only grip I have on my temper.
Have yourself a merry little Christmas-
Don't worry about the mess; I'll clean it up, I guess.

24 December 2020

weekend

I can't think of wildfire without tasting your name
On my tongue and lingering against my lips
Morning coffee and wild laughter and breathless darkness
A blurred symphony,
kaleidoscope revelry- you and me,
Embers dancing in the stirring breeze

They don't ask about you and I try to pretend it doesn't hurt
But the thing is my throat aches and so do my thighs
And I'll take my private blaze
Over prying eyes and prying minds anyway

I can't think of wildfire without tasting your name
And wildfire is the only thing dancing through my brain today

3 January 2021

nye

I won't make it till midnight
10:59
and I'm already in this usually-empty bed of mine
tonight there's a man in it
we've already done some sinning
might do some more before the sunrise
but for now he's asleep and soon so will be I
midnight's too late and I hated this year anyway,
so if I don't see this day end and the next one begin
well- fuck 2020, that's what we all say
10:59
his skin warm against mine
I'd rather close my eyes than try to watch the minutes pass by
I won't make it till midnight
but that's alright with me

                                                            31 December 2020

10:12 [I'm on the couch which isn't where I should be]

I'm too tired to be scrolling mindlessly
through images of line work tattoos and crimson starfish

I'm too content to hang up the phone
Even when the voice on the other end falls silent

4 January 2021

Devils never sinned as pure as this

I'm too mortal to be holy,
Too aware of my own ending to care for austere eternity.
Like the cresting of a wave or the flash of lightening in the sky,
The power peaks right before its destruction
And I crave the reckless free-fall
That's born each time you say my name and dies
With each final shuddering sigh.

22 December 2020

Fucking Casanova

There's a man
Says he doesn't want anything but my time
I don't know what that's like
But I might try to figure out my life
His voice in my ears at night
Sometimes neither of us say anything
And I don't know why he likes to listen to me complain
But he's a mix of sympathy and 'poor thing'
That works bizarrely
I'm not used to someone being good
He must want something from me
But right now, he just lets me breathe

23 December 2020

I'd Rather Be on A Beach in Florida

There's frost on the windowpane
                                    (Real life is intruding again today
                             Lists and tasks spinning around my brain)
I woke up alone between my sheets,
But at least they were clean-
                                  (I think he might be good for me
                           But last week wasn't reality and I'm worried
                                        He'll hate the real me)
I'm settling back into routine
Coffee cup, Netflix stuff, write before the kids get up
                                          (He's nine hours away
                                Back to his own regular day-to-day)
I wish reality didn't have to stay

                                                        4 January 2021

there are more things in heaven and earth

I believe in him like I believe in ghosts,
Spirits clinging to this world like I'd cling
to his hand if pride and distance would let me.

He's fire when he's here
And haunts me when he's gone-
> *The scent of him hanging from my shoulders*
> *The heat of his palm lingering embers on my cheek*
> *The taste of his name ashes on my tongue*

I believe in him like I believe in the phoenix,
Because *I rise, I rise, I rise*
From the coals at the sound of his voice-
A lovely ghost in my headphones
Until he possesses me again.

9 January 2021

Before you cut your bangs

You need to ask yourself if you've really tried
All there is to try and this is the last option-

Did you stare directly into the sun until you saw spots on your vision
And searched them for meaning like some fucked-up Rorschach test?
Did you dye your hair day-glo orange and paint your lips purple,
Rip holes in your jeans and holes in your skin,
Pouring your ass into too-tight pants and your feelings onto the pages of a diary
You desperately hoped someone would read but no one would ever find?
Did you ask the stars why with tears on your face in the middle of the night
And beg the rising sun to give you insight into
What to do next?

Did you come to the desperate conclusion
That you need to either end yourself
Or cut your hair?

If the answer's yes- you got that piercing
And then healed the infection and sobbed on your
Best friend's couch for an hour over board games and tequila shots-
And you're looking from the razor to the scissors

Then please know,
The bangs will look amazing on you.

11 January 2021

i try to die but i keep winning every fight

I wish it didn't start with you-

These blood-soaked cigarettes still burn
Just another regret and another vice
I'm outside beneath a street lamp at midnight
Hoping someone takes the bait
Violence in my face but fear in my mind

Does it hurt to die? Does it hurt to cry?

I wish it didn't end with you-

Bruises and scrapes and tattered knuckles,
Tired eyes tired muscles tired souls in dirty rooms
It's over too soon, cash on the table and another cigarette
Sweat going cold and they all said "you're so young" but I feel old
My bones are broken but my heart is worse, it's still pumping
Blood in my veins blood on my shirt bloody lip
And bloody cigarettes in my back pocket
I miss your hand in it and that's why I'm here again-

It all comes back to you.

27 January 2021

Bad Guys Do It Better Too

I told you I wanted a storybook love
And you assumed I wanted a hero-
But the hero puts the world before himself
And I will never be second place.
Love me like the villain would, whole heart,
Nothing held back- set the world on fire
Just to see the way my eyes shine in the blaze.

6 February 2021

it seems I can be a poet and happy

>*When you met me I was covered in moss;*
>*All roots and decay dreaming of being a star*

I don't write poetry anymore;
I can't remember what's like to lie motionless for hours
And imagine broken things and broken dreams

>*I am no longer embedded in the earth*
>*I have risen from the moss and the rot and the dreams*
>*Now I am weightless and moving, a dance of sunlight*
>*And starlight, comet of endless flame-*

Now I'm writing poetry again;
Scratching lyrics into the skyline and
Leaving my footprints on sun-drenched lines

5 March 2021

new beginnings are not always beautiful

I think I will sit and stare at this white wall for hours
There are holes and chips where framed portraits used to hang,
Evidence that the blankness is hard-won and battered
I can prop my feet on the wall and admire what I've done in the silence
Of this empty house l celebrate instead of shun
There is a difference between blank and empty
There is a difference between lonely and alone

14 March 2021

Writer's Block & Sunrise

The words are bottled up
A lump in my throat I cannot force past the pen
Burnt stars are coal too and maybe I can write
My heart in the sky,
but maybe it's too much
For the galaxy to contain, like the white paper
Mocking my efforts and my tears
In the end it isn't the stars I want
Or the endless black of the night sky;
It's the daybreak, the dawn, the glow of gold on the horizon
And the glow of gold filling my skin
It isn't coal; it's the warmth of the flame

16 April 2021

[wait for a love like the myths]

Persephone selects a pomegranate seed
With delicate fingers and painted lips
Salivating boys watch each bite
Aching for her to be stolen, duped-
But Hades knew that Spring ends and plants wither
And he counted the seeds himself
Before presenting her the fruit.

                                                  20 April 2021

"I love you, Mr. Mom!"

I bought my favorite coffee mug in a thrift store
For $.50 two months after I asked my ex to move out.
My second Mother's Day as a single mom
I sip semi-cold coffee as I listen to my children tell me
All about the show they watch on their tablets
At their father's house.
We howl like wolves and roar like lions, wild and silly,
And two blonde heads and four laughing blue eyes
Shine brighter than the gold of my thrift-store mug.
I'd rather have this than forced affection and expensive gifts.

9 May 2021

scapegoat

They say
    Pain travels through families
        Until someone is ready to feel it
I've felt my share but I
    wasn't ready,
        wasn't ready,
            wasn't ready
                (Ready steady go)
Do scapegoats have horns or
    Are they shorn of all their weapons when
           They're chosen?
    (Was I chosen?)
Is there choice when you're the sacrifice
    (Can you burn before the pain hurts twice?)
They say
        (I can't remember)
    They say
        They say
            It runs through families

12 June 2021

The things that hurt (I'm a little bit off today)

Tonight I grow tired thinking of the things that hurt
Like how the hem of his shirt I wear to bed grazes my thighs
Right above where there used to be thin red lines
(A decade ago, but fresh in my mind) or
The bruise below my knee that only serves as a reminder
Of how easy it is bruise every part of me
(Haven't you heard this story?)
{Once upon a time I lay on my back and tried
To step outside my own mind;
Once upon a time I looked through pictures not
Comprehending what I might find;
Once upon a time I worked through the chaos
One sting of pain at a time}
Now I lay on my back in my bed, phone next to my head
And I tell him the things that hurt instead

16 June 2021

Zombie

I forgot to tell my body the day I died
Walking corpse, puppet-like moving through time
I forgot to tell my body the day I was reborn
Settling back into the decayed crevasses of my mind
Sometimes my body knows things before I do
Knows when to kill me and when to bring me back
To myself, fresh and whole and new,
Despite the scars and the rotten places
I forgot to tell my body I was dying,
But it forgot to tell me I needed you.

22 June 2021

The God Thieves

    There is a reason they tell you never steal from the divine

Immortality is a poison drug dragging through your veins
                {Exhilaration and starvation}

Godhood a trudge up an endless mountain
Never peaking never falling never ceasing

      {I can't remember what time felt like
      When we were afraid of losing it
      I can't remember what death was like
      Though I'm constantly longing to taste it}

When we took the cup and sipped we never imagined
We would drown in it;

                We only wanted more time
(now we long for the end of it.)

                                    12 September 2021

skin deep

Sometimes I wonder

        When I stopped wearing makeup-

Was it when I realized

        The world has bigger problems

Than what I put on my face,

        Or that I do?

        30 June 2021

scientifically speaking, maybe we are soul mates

You cannot gain cold;
There is only an absence of heat.
Maybe that's why I'm drawn to the flames
      & to the sun
           & to you.

10 December 2021

Something in the Water

They say your ribs are a cage
Mine are an octopus, tentacles wrapping my heart
To hold it secure in the ocean of my body
But it is a soft, living thing
Too easily moving aside to let others in
I should teach it to be a jellyfish
To sting all who come close
But I can't change what lives within me any more
Than I can change the moon's pull on the tides
So there is something in the waters of my body
That even I can't tame.

17 October 2021

Part IV:

the mythology of [you + me]

say something dangerous, like 'I love you'
-anne sexton, the complete poems of anne sexton, from "the papa and
mama dance"

Healing

He talks dirty to me and it doesn't make me flinch
I used to hate the way the word [cock] sounded
Almost as much as the way one felt hitting the back of my throat
Now I'm on my knees willingly
Not a supplicant but a goddess granting a wish
My name a prayer from his lips and his hands in my hair
I never imagined I'd fuck like this
No shields, no walls
My body melting into his hands, following his commands
He talks forever to me and it doesn't make me tense
The future assured in his mind because everything is
I hate the word [promises] because an unbroken one doesn't exist
Funny thing is I believe them coming from his lips
Each time he says I'm it for him, all there is
I never thought I could love like this,
No walls, no guards
Heart in his hands, daydreams following his plans
I don't know what this is if it isn't healing
I don't know what happy is if this isn't it

27 July 2021

scurvy

My mouth is full of strawberries
(Is this the taste of love?)
Summer fruit or well-kissed lipstick, it looks the same
The corners of my mouth red-smeared and messy-
Blueberries dye my fingertips
Less blue than purple but it reminds me
Of the blood flowing back to your heart
(Lack of oxygen turns it the color of my eyes;
maybe that's why I'm so lightheaded around you)
Spiderweb veins in your arms patterns I memorize
Fingers gliding over skin and soft sighs
(You take the offered bite; I laugh when you roll your eyes)
Summer stains me everywhere
(or is that you?)

15 June 2021

all that glitters in the dark

Somewhere, the night sky is a tapestry of diamonds
Darkness never bothered me and shadows give me peace
But maybe what we need is the opposite of what we seek
I think my deepest thoughts as I drift to sleep,
Not on my knees, praying to gods I don't believe in
Diamonds are just rocks that thrived in heat
Stars are just gases that burned up in space
Thousands of miles away from this place, away
From the questions that haunt my dreams-
Maybe I'm nothing but stardust and need
Maybe I'm wishing for terrible things
Maybe diamonds and darkness are more than they seem

6 June 2021

My father taught me to be tough

I flick my knife open and closed absently just like my father-
Mind elsewhere, fingers busy
        (This war I'm fighting will bring me to my knees)
The first time I learned to measure and weigh words
Was listening to him and my mother fight
        (I am covered in bleeding wounds and
        Long-healed scars, but I am. I am.)
I delivered a perfect heel strike to an already-crumbling bookcase
And wished he was there to be proud of me when it collapsed.
When I sobbed until I fell asleep instead of breaking
The glass bottle still in my hand,
I wondered if he would be proud of that too.
        (I am. I am. I am.)

7 May 2021

2 Weeks

It's been too long since you were here
The muscles at the base of my neck are tense,
Body drawn taunt, a bent bowstring
      (I always think of my body in terms of weapons;
      Living is a war, and I am determined to win.
      Sex, love, life- they're all just battles.)
My back will be locked before you touch me
And all the knots will untie,
Tension draining from my limbs like rivers to the sea.
      (I always think of you in terms of safety-
      Armor, fortress, rock; weapons laid down and gentle-
      touching hands.
      Living is war, but when the battle is over-
            You're there.)

                                        16 March 2021

tiny pagans

My children whisper gratitudes
Small fingers touching beads carefully,
Intent on this new thing I've shown them,
Intent on creating the good energy I've said they can raise.

They tell me that the sun moving behind clouds
Is playing hide-and-seek, wide-eyed and innocent
And full of the power I am just learning to recreate.

Sometimes,
I am not the one who makes the magic.
Sometimes,
I learn it from them.

7 July 2021

early morning

arm around my waist, heavy and warm
rhythmic breathing against my hip
the steady cadence of the words as I turn pages
lost in another world while grounded in this
against soft sheets and warm skin

10 July 2021

late-night murder spree

It's 2am
And we're in my kitchen laughing, fly swatters in hand
I've always believed nothing good happens after midnight
(How did I get this lucky?)
Sometimes what you've always believed isn't always right
New moon can be the brightest light after all
And maybe when it's 2am you and I fall into
Each other more than ever.
I think it makes us better when
It's 2am
And I won't pretend I'm the same as I was
Last time I stayed up this late-
Pushing midnight or pushing fate, I've found out
Happiness doesn't wait around for me to tame
So at 2am
I'm laughing with you again.

12 July 2021

Lies I told when I thought you wouldn't notice

It's strange that my bed doesn't feel too small when you're in it
           {I don't like to be touched when I'm sleeping}
I curl around you if you aren't curled around me already,
Heat-seeking missiles, fire to fire
           {I don't like morning sex}
Turns out I love waking up beside you,
Love long mornings in bed, your face against my hip,
Coffee in hand, till your fingers creep up my thigh
and I'm laughing, then gasping
               {I don't want a relationship}
I want a forever, I want a partner,
I want your ring on my finger
               {I'm done having children}
Maybe I can be a mother again, if you promise to kiss my swelling stomach
And slide your fingers up my thighs after lazy coffee-sweet mornings
And curl around me in the night in the bed that should be too small with you in it
But somehow isn't
               My god, I never knew I was such a liar
      {I wouldn't trust me either}

                                        15 July 2021

Unburdened [atlas couldn't shrug]

The first time I saw him
He hunched even as he smiled
I stood on my toes and still barely reached to hold on tight
My god you're tall- he laughed
[I think his shoulders hunched more]
Something holds him down
[gravity or maybe force of will]
So he doesn't fly away or rival the mountains to touch the heights
I'd buy him a one-way ticket anywhere
To see him standing straight, head high
[No one thinks of Atlas as tall if we think of him at all
But if we took the sky from his shoulders
I think he would probably be
Just a man]

27 August 2021

the sea gives me dead things

I've been picking up
broken pieces of luck
these sand dollar dreams have always been enough
tides push and tides pull,
something burrows in my tired soul
a broken fragment of a dream that was whole
[maybe someday I'll be whole]
I tell myself I will glue them back together
gold-painted cracks and forced control
in these small, shattered parts of a once-living home
but I hold broken luck in my hand
and the shape of a sand dollar's bones
is more beautiful to me when it's in pieces
than when it's whole-
luck is what we make of it after all
[maybe it's me who was always whole]

25 September 2021

your mother is a witch

Everyone knows your mother is a witch
    You hear the whispers as you walk the street
        See the curled lips and crosses
Everyone knows witch-spawn is evil
    Daughter of demons
        Dances with the devil and holds him tight
Everyone knows you ride the sky at night
    Broom-bristles and cats in moonlight
        Black hat societies and poisonous plants
Everyone knows
    Everyone knows
        Everyone knows
            (What's different must be bad.)

                        27 September 2021

lavender ghosts

Replace the scent of him with lavender soap.
    I never mind it clinging to my skin;
        like him, I don't want it to go,
    But I think my boss might mind
If my hair's a mess and I smell like sex.
    So he's on the road and I'll wash the sheets
        And the towels and the dishes and the clothes.
    These lavender flowers will linger like his ghost.
My body aches from the sex and the water's gone cold-
    Lavender only covers so much, you know.

                                3 October 2021

Home

I remember
5:30 in December, unfamiliar car in my driveway
Couldn't believe you'd driven 11 hours to me
Cold air on Christmas morning
I opened the door and called you crazy
Hands in my pockets and heart pounding
You walked in, closed the door, and I'll never forget
The way the world shifted and I steadied
When I leaned against your shoulder
First time I let you hold me
I've never felt anything like that morning
And your shoulder under my forehead-
I straightened up because if I stayed I'd have started crying
And now I know that feeling I couldn't name then.

13 October 2021

Playlist

Some days when I can't believe I'm loved
Those opening notes start playing in my mind
And I remember all the times you send me
Screenshots of songs as you drive.
On the road with a playlist sixty songs long
No one can be loved more than like a country love song.

13 October 2021

[don't worry; I got it]

Sometimes I'll stretch out in my bed
And hate that I can reach to either side, fingers
Only finding empty sheets while
I'm trying to empty my mind
There's a price for having it all how you want it
[There's a price for everything, and I know how to pay it]
Maybe someday I'll run out of ways to purchase independence
But I know how to stretch a dollar and how to fill
Every corner of an empty bed and empty
Everything from my head but my own will,
My own dreams
I'll touch opposite corners as long as it takes
To live in peace in my own space.

21 July 2021

there is no cursing in the dojo

I take karate with a handful of manly men-
Retired cops, upper black belts, the kind
Who pride themselves on being the baddest in the room.
    I'm tougher than all of them.
They'll hit their knees and yell
Pain a tangible thing long before they'll tap out
And let it end.
                      They say
    It's just my youth
        Or my joints
             Or the way my body bends
That keeps me silent when they yell.
    (Truth is,
I'm stronger than them.)
    The truth is,
I've been through hell
            And there is nothing
All these manly men can do that touches where I've been.

                                6 July 2021

dancing on my graves

They say each birth mark shows a way you died-
If that is true I am no longer surprised
By the small brown mark between my thighs.
Sometimes I wonder if every woman I meet is scarred
If we all bear the same mark
Universal death written on our most intimate parts.
I laugh when someone gestures to my shoulder
'They say birthmarks show how you died'
(You never know what the map of my skin hides.)

1 July 2021

over and over

Even when it's over it isn't really over
Lying on my back, stomach sticky and wet,
I think I was in shock but I didn't know it yet
Can't remember what he cleaned me off with that day
(I think it was my shirt? Wouldn't have been his, no way)
I wasn't humiliated then, just in pain and out of my own brain
Hours go by and I'd try to cut it from my mind
But all I found was skin
A few months later and there I was again
Cold floor under my back,
      cold sticky stomach,
            Cold numb body and brain
I remember it was dark and he was looking for the exit
Cleaned up with paper towels but my shirt got wet
(The shower helped, so did the blood)
Fast-forward
     blurred lines
         blurred moments in time
His grip tight when I was unsteady
Slammed into my body until he was ready,
Flip to my back and I'm once again sticky
(He stole a shirt to clean me up; never would dirty something of his)
Even when it's over it isn't over
There's always the clean up
(I think I'm going to be cleaning up his mess for the rest of my life)

17 October 2021

Rorschach

Sometimes I wonder if I'm anything more than an ink stain,
Someone else's cryptic words on blank paper
Attempting to write into being the pain they feel inside
Sometimes I question the verity of reality-
Is everything I am, and everything I see,
Nothing more than a figment of someone else's dreams?
    (Can my pen create more than it seems?)

21 October 2021

viviere

Pomegranate drips down the back of my throat
(Heavy as *fuck*, sticky-sweet as *forever*)
Wine-red stains can be washed from porcelain cups
And coffee brought to me in bed is sweeter anyway
Peach-soft sunlight and dusty dawn glow on skin
Against mine, softer than sheets, arms stronger than
Rug-covered floors under my knees and heaven between my teeth-
(I still have a mouth made for sinning;
I still leave stains and fire arrows)
Rosy-hued and wine-dark blend together
When held in balance
(*Asshole* and *always* never before sounded the same)
Midnight whisky and morning coffee burn bitter in different ways
But what I stain can be cleaned; what I need I can claim.

3 November 2021

7 December [if only in my dreams]

Plug in the tree, sip my coffee
It's 6:30 am again, 7th of December
And I'm trying to remember just when this season
Stop being magic and started being stress
Why can't I just relax, enjoy the chaos, enjoy the mess?
What I remember best wasn't the shopping or the rush
It's the laughs and the lights and I'm trying to get that right
But somehow I'm singing along to a wistful song
About coming home in my dreams and I wonder
When Christmas will be what I remember
But I'm sipping coffee at 6:30 on the 7th of December
And I know it's up to me to recreate those scenes
For the two boys who are asleep
So I plugged in the tree.

7 December 2021

merry [let your heart be light]

There is something about the glow of a Christmas tree
That makes me want to write
Wistful and beautiful and magic and heartache all at once
In a soft colored glow that reflects
on my early-morning mug and my wandering thoughts.
The windows are dark, longest night of the year
Not yet ended
New beginnings and new endings and bright happy lights
Reflecting back into my eyes
And I wonder if everyone feels this way sometimes
Like the merry and bright is brittle but
None of us want it to be so we struggle to make it magic-
Maybe I'm just getting older, caught between
The cynicism and the way the lights look in little boys smiles
My Christmas tree makes it look as though one outside my window
Is twinkling colors and sometimes I think that's
How we all feel as we try to do it right-
A reflection of the joy, a mirror for the magic
But somehow I think that's alright.

22 December 2021

medication meditations

He said {I don't need my sleep medicine
When I'm sleeping next you}
The words coated the back of my throat like guilt
The sickly-sweet of a melatonin gummy and the burning bitter
Of anxiety pills on my tongue
It gnawed at my mind till I looked him in the eyes
{I love you, but you don't cure my crazy}
      (I'm sorry you can't make me sleep
      I'm sorry you don't calm my worries
      I'm sorry I can't say you complete me-
      I'm a whole person by myself, damage and all)
Quick laugh, easy acceptance
      {I know}

28 December 2021

countdown *[3, 2, 1]*

One of my friends spent $250 on a bottle of booze.
I'm cutting down my grocery bill, no more fast food-
I'm rubbing pennies together until they cry.
(Is it worth my money?
Is it worth my time?)
Someday I won't be counting quarters and dimes,
Someday I'll have everything, money and time and
I'll be counting the books I've read and the hours I've slept
Not the moments I have left before the next task begins,
Not the dollars I haven't got to spend-
I can stretch myself and stretch the cash
I can nod my head when they spend $250 and laugh.
(Truth is, I'm never going to be like that.)

31 December 2021

if you aren't part of the solution you're part of the problem

    There's an amber alert on the billboard outside my hometown

One of my friends is drunk and calling for anarchy at
9 in the morning, lamenting the lack of personal freedom
    When their inconvenience and discomfort can save a life
        And I'm wondering why I'm trying so hard to make sense
    To someone who wants to be senseless-

Last night I argued feminism with a man
    Determined not to understand the need for it

And this morning I'm pulling into work despite the way my body still hurts

But I'm out of sick leave and human beings stopped being
    More important than the smooth running of the machine
      A long while back.

[God, I'm so tired of this world and all the battles in it]

I want to look at those around me and ask them
    When did you start hating yourself so much
        That now you can't see the worth in others?
    When did you start believing that you weren't worth saving?

[And is that why no one else is?]

                                7 January 2022

slumbering haze

                                            [*father's anger*
                            father's anger
            father's anger-]

all the world revolves around our father's anger

            but I have the rage of my mother
when my temper is roused, hotter than coal
 redder than the blood
      between my legs
          between my teeth
              [coating my tongue]

[how often must we revolve around the matchstick anger of
fathers
when it is the weighty rage of generations that
stirs heavy in the hearts
                deep in the cores
         of the dormant volcanoes of mothers?]

                                            7 January 2022

Car ride, Jan. 18th {*dreams deferred*}

We talk about the moon's phases
Full and new and why her face will change.
The boys have a solar system model at their father's
And I confess that once I dreamed of being out among the stars.
My oldest asks if I can still be an astronaut,
And I laugh, that dream long gone-
But he sounds so sad when I say no and he asks why not,
And I remember what it's like to learn that dreams can die.
But I'm not sad I never left this earth,
Cause gravity might weigh me down but regrets can't.
We talk about the dreams I've achieved,
The ones I'm still trying to reach,
And he tells me he's decided he's going
To be everything when he grows up,
Everything he's ever dreamed, all at once.
I tell him that's exactly what he should do,
Then we talk Transformers under the full moon.

18 January 2022

Tales

No story is just a story
There is something of the author in every telling,
Some secret of heart or mind or longing
Slipped between the letters
Dripping through the words
Dancing in the white spaces and mingling with the ink
No story is just a story
[Can you leave yourself on the page and never look back?]

11 January 2022